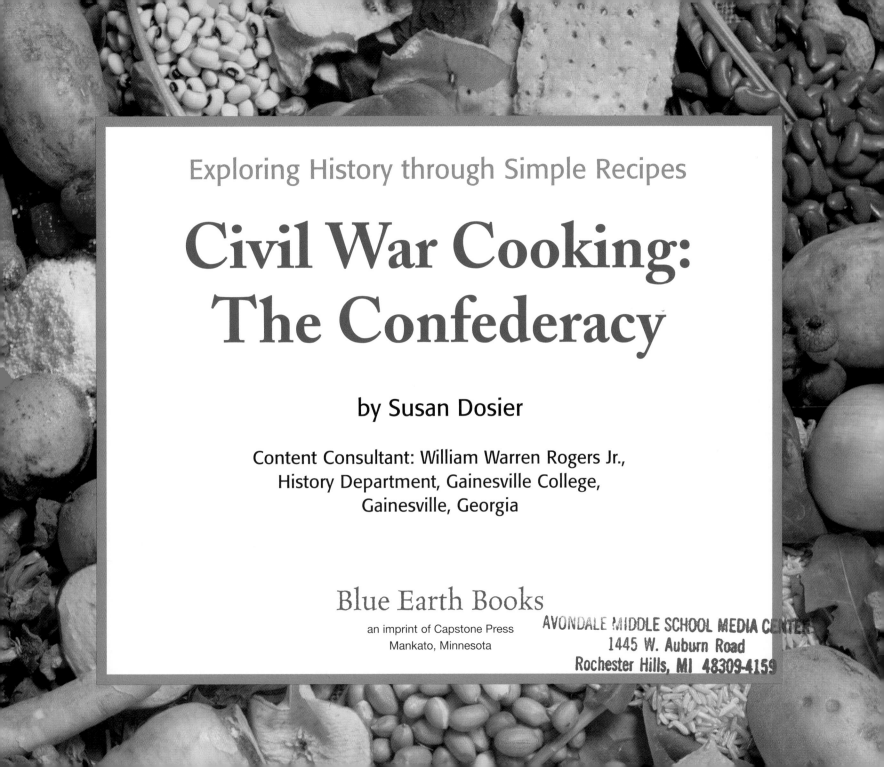

Exploring History through Simple Recipes

Civil War Cooking: The Confederacy

by Susan Dosier

Content Consultant: William Warren Rogers Jr.,
History Department, Gainesville College,
Gainesville, Georgia

Blue Earth Books

an imprint of Capstone Press
Mankato, Minnesota

Blue Earth Books are published by Capstone Press
151 Good Counsel Drive, P.O. Box 669, Mankato, Minnesota 56002
http://www.capstone-press.com

Library of Congress Cataloging-in-Publication Data
Dosier, Susan.
　　Civil War cooking: The Confederacy/ by Susan Dosier.
　　p. cm.—(Exploring history through simple recipes)
　　Summary: Discusses the everyday life, cooking methods, foods, and celebrations of Confederate soldiers during the Civil War. Includes recipes and sidebars.
　　ISBN 0-7368-0350-5
　　1. Cookery, American—History Juvenile literature. 2. United States—History—Civil War, 1861-1865 Juvenile literature. [1. Cookery, American—History. 2. United States—History—Civil War, 1861-1865.] I. Title. II. Series.
TX715.D6874 2000
641.5973'09034—dc21
99-20749
CIP

Editorial credits

Editor, Kay M. Olson; cover designer, Steve Christensen; interior designer, Heather Kindseth; illustrator, Linda Clavel; photo researchers, Kimberly Danger and Katy Kudela.

Acknowledgments

Blue Earth Books thanks the following children who helped test recipes: John Christensen, Matthew Christensen, Maerin Coughlan, Beth Goebel, Nicole Hilger, Abby Rothenbuehler, Alice Ruff, Hannah Schoof, and Molly Wandersee.

Photo credits

North Wind Picture Archives, cover, 8, 10, 12, 14, 18; Gregg Andersen, cover (background) and recipes, 11, 13, 15, 19, 23, 28; Archive Photos, 7, 20; Library of Congress, 17, 25, 29; Museum of the Confederacy, 21; Corbis-Bettmann, 23.

Editor's note

Adult supervision may be needed for some recipes in this book. All recipes have been tested. Although based on historical foods, recipes have been modernized and simplified for today's young cooks.

1 2 3 4 5 6 05 04 03 02 01 00

2/02　$15.73　World Almanac

Contents

Metric Conversion Guide

U.S.	Canada
¼ teaspoon	1 mL
½ teaspoon	2 mL
1 teaspoon	5 mL
1 tablespoon	15 mL
¼ cup	50 mL
⅓ cup	75 mL
½ cup	125 mL
⅔ cup	150 mL
¾ cup	175 mL
1 cup	250 mL
1 quart	1 liter
1 ounce	30 grams
2 ounces	55 grams
4 ounces	85 grams
½ pound	225 grams
1 pound	455 grams

Fahrenheit	Celsius
325 degrees	160 degrees
350 degrees	180 degrees
375 degrees	190 degrees
400 degrees	200 degrees
425 degrees	220 degrees

Kitchen Safety

1. Make sure your hair and clothes will not be in the way while you are cooking.

2. Keep a fire extinguisher in the kitchen. Never put water on a grease fire.

3. Wash your hands with soap before you start to cook. Wash your hands with soap again after you handle meat or poultry.

4. Ask an adult for help with sharp knives, the stove, the oven, and all electrical appliances.

5. Turn handles of pots and pans to the middle of the stove. A person walking by could run into handles that stick out toward the room.

6. Use dry pot holders to take dishes out of the oven.

7. Wash all fruits and vegetables.

8. Always use a clean cutting board. Wash the cutting board thoroughly after cutting meat or poultry.

9. Wipe up spills immediately.

10. Store leftovers properly. Do not leave leftovers out at room temperature for more than two hours.

Cooking Equipment

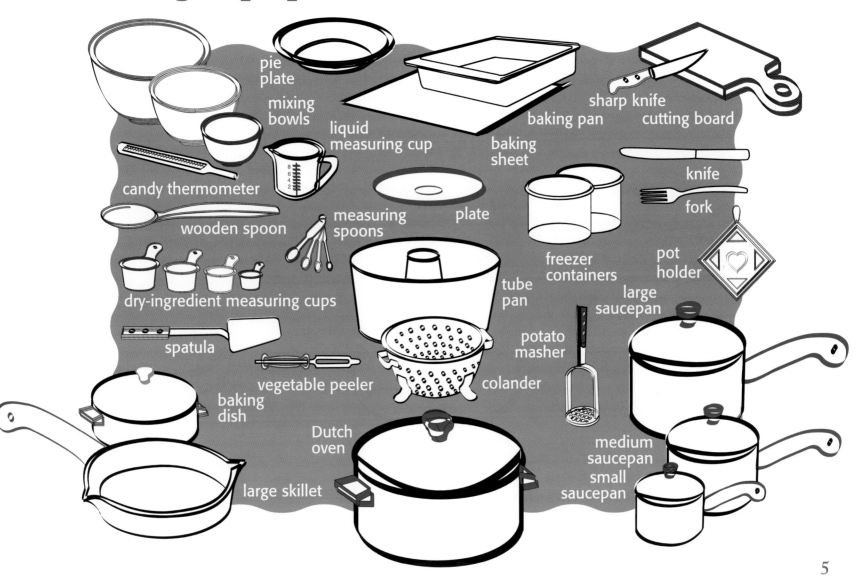

pie plate

mixing bowls

liquid measuring cup

baking pan

sharp knife

cutting board

baking sheet

candy thermometer

knife

measuring spoons

plate

fork

wooden spoon

freezer containers

pot holder

tube pan

large saucepan

dry-ingredient measuring cups

potato masher

spatula

vegetable peeler

colander

baking dish

Dutch oven

medium saucepan

small saucepan

large skillet

The Civil War

In 1860, many differences divided the United States. Southerners believed in a strong state government, and Northerners believed in a strong national government. Southerners were loyal to their individual states and felt each state had the right to make its own laws. Northerners felt most political and social issues should be the federal government's business.

Other differences separated the North and the South. In the North, people had small farms or worked in businesses and factories. The South was one of the world's leading suppliers of cotton. Southern plantation owners used slaves to grow and pick the cotton. Picking cotton was hot, hard work. Owners provided food and shelter for their slaves but gave them little else. Slavery was part of the traditional way of life in the South.

The North and the South also disagreed about slavery in new states that were joining the Union. In 1820, the government passed a law called the Missouri Compromise that banned slavery in the northern territories. Southern leaders feared that every time a new state joined the Union, the South would lose power in the government. When Abraham Lincoln ran for president in 1860, he promised to outlaw slavery in all new states and territories.

When Lincoln won the election, Southerners believed their way of life was being threatened. They decided that the time had come for them to leave the United States to form their own government. By 1861, 11 of the Southern states had seceded from the United States. These states set up their own government called the Confederate States of America.

U.S. soldiers were serving at Fort Sumter when South Carolina seceded from the Union. Southerners believed the fort belonged to the Confederacy. In April, 1861, Union troops at Fort Sumter ran out of supplies. Southerners thought the

The Confederate Army had about 1.5 million soldiers when the Civil War started in 1861. One-fourth of these Confederate soldiers were dead when the Civil War ended in 1865.

**Sell your books at
sellbackyourBook.com!**
Go to sellbackyourBook.com
and get an instant price
quote. We even pay the
shipping - see what your old
books are worth today!

Inspected By: Daniel _sillas

00045738382

8382

0004573   L

soldiers would leave the fort when they faced starvation. But President Lincoln wanted the Union to stay together. He ordered federal ships to bring food and supplies to the Union troops at Fort Sumter. This action was the trigger for war. On April 12, 1861, Confederate soldiers fired on the Union troops at Fort Sumter. These shots started the Civil War (1861-1865).

The long war caused many problems for the South. The U.S. Navy set up blockades near Southern port cities. This barrier of ships kept food and supplies from reaching the Southern states. Union soldiers damaged Southern railroads, making it difficult to transport food to towns and battlefields. Both the Confederate soldiers and their families back home often went hungry.

The Union won the Civil War. Confederate General Robert E. Lee surrendered to Union General Ulysses S. Grant in 1865. Only three-fourths of the Confederate soldiers survived the war. The others died in battle or of illness. About 620,000 Confederate and Union soldiers died from battle or disease during the Civil War. More soldiers died in the Civil War than in all other U.S. wars combined.

Slaves and the Emancipation Proclamation

The Confederate Army did not admit slaves as soldiers. But some Confederate soldiers took their slaves with them to war. Male slaves repaired the railroads that Northern troops destroyed. Slaves also looked after Confederate soldiers in Southern hospitals.

On January 1, 1863, President Abraham Lincoln declared that slaves in the states opposing the Union were free. This declaration was called the Emancipation Proclamation.

The Emancipation Proclamation did not immediately free any slaves. The 3.5 million slaves in the South gained their freedom when the Union won the Civil War in 1865. Slavery in the United States officially ended in December 1865 with the adoption of the Thirteenth Amendment to the U.S. Constitution. After the war, most Southern slaves still farmed for a living. Many worked for their former owners. They received wages or a share of the crops in exchange for their labor.

The South and the North, 1861–1865

Southern states were called the Confederacy. The Confederacy required white men between the ages of 18 and 35 to join the army. Southern soldiers were called Confederates or Rebels. A nickname for a Southern soldier was Johnny Reb. The Confederate Army numbered about 1.5 million. Soldiers wore gray uniforms.

The Northern states were called the Union. Northern soldiers were called Federals or Yankees. Billy Yank was a nickname for a Union soldier. Almost 3 million soldiers served in the Union Army. They wore blue uniforms.

Minnesota
Wisconsin
Michigan
Iowa
Illinois
Indiana
Ohio
Missouri
Kentucky
Kansas
Tennessee
Arkansas
Mississippi
Georgia
Alabama
Texas
Louisiana
Florida
West Virginia
Virginia
North Carolina
South Carolina
New Hampshire
Vermont
Maine
Massachusetts
New York
Rhode Island
Connecticut
Pennsylvania
New Jersey
Delaware
Maryland

Atlantic Ocean

Gulf of Mexico

■ Union States
□ Border States
■ Confederate States

Rations for Johnny Reb

The Confederate Army handed out rations to the soldiers. Soldiers often traded or shared rations with each other. The soldiers usually ate their rations in groups of four to eight men. They took turns cooking over campfires. Some groups did not have pans for cooking. They used hoes or corn husks as makeshift pans, or they ate their food cold.

The Confederacy often did not have enough food to feed its soldiers. Soldiers had to search for extra food on their own. Some soldiers hunted in the forests or looked for berries and other foods that grew wild. Soldiers sometimes bought food from local farmers. Other soldiers stole food.

Soldiers who were marching or fighting often went hungry for days. The soldiers had to make do with food they could carry. Confederate soldiers depended on hardtack. These hard crackers made from flour, salt, and water did not spoil. Although most Union and Confederate soldiers did not like hardtack, it did have some advantages. Hardtack was light, which made it easy to carry. The crackers contained a great deal of salt. The salt helped the soldiers to sweat, which kept them from fainting in the hot summer months.

Soldiers gave hardtack names like "iron plate biscuits" and "teeth dullers" because it was so tough. Soldiers also called hardtack "worm castle" because the crackers often contained bugs. Weevils and maggots burrowed into the hardtack.

The hungry soldiers found many ways to eat hardtack. They dipped hardtack in water, coffee, or tea. This practice helped soften the hardtack so it did not break the soldiers' teeth. If the coffee or tea was hot enough, it also would kill the bugs. Other soldiers ate unsoftened hardtack after breaking it into small pieces with the ends of their guns. Soldiers sometimes fried hardtack in pork fat.

Confederate soldiers had to make do with food they could carry on long marches. Hardtack was a good choice because it was light and did not spoil.

Hardtack

WARNING: DO NOT eat hardtack without first dipping it into milk or hot chocolate. Hardtack may break your teeth if you eat it dry.

Ingredients
1 tablespoon butter or margarine for
   greasing
5 cups all-purpose flour
1 tablespoon baking powder
1 tablespoon salt
1⅔ cups water

Equipment
baking sheet
paper towel or napkin
dry-ingredient measuring cups
measuring spoons
liquid measuring cup
wooden spoon
table knife   pot holders
toothpick   spatula

1. Preheat oven to 450°F (240°C). Use a paper towel or napkin dabbed with 1 tablespoon butter or margarine to lightly grease baking sheet.
2. In bowl, combine 5 cups flour, 1 tablespoon baking powder, 1 tablespoon salt, and 1⅔ cups water. Stir mixture with wooden spoon. Wash your hands, then squeeze the hardtack mixture with your fingers. The dough will be very stiff.
3. Flatten the dough with your hands to a ½-inch (1.25-centimeter) thickness on the baking sheet. Shape dough into a large rectangle.
4. Use knife to lightly trace lines into dough to divide it into nine 3-inch by 3-inch (7.6-centimeter by 7.6-centimeter) square pieces.
5. Use toothpick to prick holes across the entire surface of the dough. The holes should be made all the way through the dough to the baking sheet.
6. Bake 25 minutes or until lightly browned.
7. Let cool 10 minutes. Remove from the baking sheet with a metal spatula.

Makes 9 crackers

Counting on Cornmeal

Many foods were scarce during the Civil War. White flour was hard to find. People had to try other ingredients in bread. Soldiers' rations often contained coarsely ground corn called cornmeal. Cornmeal regularly took the place of flour for both Southern soldiers and Southern families.

Soldiers used cornmeal in many ways. They combined cornmeal, water, and salt. They then placed the mixture on hoe blades and cooked it over the fire. Soldiers called this bread hoe cake. Soldiers also wrapped cornmeal and water mixtures in the outer husks of corn. They baked these husks in the ashes of the campfire. Fried cornmeal was another common Civil War meal. Soldiers fried cornmeal in the shape of large cakes called pones. The rough cornmeal made pones grainy and hard to chew.

Fighting in the Cornfield

Soldiers fought the bloodiest one-day battle of the Civil War at Antietam on September 17, 1862. This battle started in Miller's Cornfield near Sharpsburg, Maryland. Confederate soldiers hid among the stalks of corn in the field. As Northern troops marched toward town, the Confederates rose up in the cornfield and fired on the Union soldiers.

By evening, 12,410 Union soldiers and 10,700 Confederate soldiers had died. More Union soldiers died, but the North won the battle. The Confederate Army had fewer men than the Union Army did.

The Battle of Antietam was General Robert E. Lee's first invasion of the North. He moved troops to the North to take advantage of the farm fields in Maryland that had not yet been harvested. Lee knew the fields held fresh food supplies for his hungry men. Lee also knew that Southern farmers could safely harvest their crops while the fighting was in the North.

Confederate Cornbread

The bread made from this recipe probably tastes better than the cornbread Confederate soldiers ate. But the ingredients are similar. This recipe uses baking powder, which makes bread light and fluffy. Confederate soldiers did not have baking powder to make cornbread. Southerners usually made cornbread with white cornmeal. If you cannot find white cornmeal in your local grocery store, use yellow cornmeal as a substitute.

Ingredients
1 tablespoon butter or margarine for greasing
2 cups white cornmeal (not self-rising)
2 teaspoons baking powder
¾ teaspoon salt
2 eggs
2 cups milk
¼ cup vegetable oil

Equipment
9-inch by 9-inch (23-centimeter by 23-centimeter) baking pan
paper towel or napkin
dry-ingredient measuring cups
measuring spoons
large bowl
wooden spoon
small bowl
fork
liquid measuring cup
pot holders

1. Preheat oven to 400° F. Use a paper towel or napkin dabbed with 1 tablespoon butter or margarine to lightly grease pan.
2. Combine 2 cups cornmeal, 2 teaspoons baking powder, and ¾ teaspoon salt in large bowl.
3. In small bowl, lightly stir 2 eggs with fork. Add to dry ingredients.
4. Add 2 cups milk and ¼ cup oil, stirring only until all ingredients are wet. Pour into pan.
5. Bake 20 to 25 minutes, or until top is lightly browned.

Makes about 9 servings

When Bread Tasted Good

Not all bread the Confederate Army provided was as rough and difficult to eat as cornbread and hardtack. Soldiers sometimes ate Sally Lunn bread in the early days of the war. Most Southern families had a recipe for Sally Lunn bread. This bread was richer and sweeter than regular bread. Ingredients for this bread included sugar and wheat flour. In the 1800s, cooks baked Sally Lunn bread in an oven warmed by a wood fire.

In the later years of the war, the ingredients to make Sally Lunn bread often were not available. Eggs were scarce and sometimes sold for $20 a dozen. Cooks used cornmeal, potatoes, or rice flour in place of wheat flour. Thinned molasses, honey, syrup, or fruit juice replaced sugar. Juice from watermelons, persimmons, and figs made Sally Lunn bread especially sweet.

Who Was Sally Lunn?

Southerners have many explanations for the name Sally Lunn. It may have been the name of a woman who sold the bread in England. Another tale says the name comes from the French language. Southerners say a French girl sold bread that was as golden as the sun. "Soleil" is the French word for sun. The bottom of the bread was as white as the moon. "Lune" is French for moon.

Soft and sweet bread was scarce in the South during the Civil War. Sally Lunn bread was only a memory for most Confederate soldiers.

Sally Lunn Bread

Ingredients

1 cup milk
1 package (2¼ teaspoons) dry yeast
½ cup (1 stick) butter
½ cup sugar
3 eggs
4 cups all-purpose flour
1 teaspoon salt
1 tablespoon butter or margarine
    for greasing

Equipment

large saucepan
liquid measuring cup
candy thermometer
2 mixing bowls
fork or hand mixer
wooden spoon
dry-ingredient measuring cups
large bowl
plastic wrap

10-inch (25-centimeter) tube pan or
    Bundt cake pan
paper towel or napkin
knife to cut bread

1. Pour 1 cup milk into saucepan. Cook over medium heat until milk begins to boil. Reduce heat and cool milk to 120°F (48°C).
2. Add 1 package yeast. Let stand 5 minutes.
3. In mixing bowl, beat ½ cup (1 stick) butter and ½ cup sugar with fork or hand mixer until mixture is light and fluffy.
4. Add 3 eggs. Beat well with fork or hand mixer.
5. In another mixing bowl, combine 4 cups flour and 1 teaspoon salt.
6. Switch off adding small amounts of flour, then milk mixture, to butter and egg mixture. Beat well after each addition. Batter will be stiff.
7. Use a paper towel or napkin dabbed with 1 tablespoon butter or margarine to grease large bowl. Place dough in bowl. Cover loosely with plastic wrap.
8. Let dough rise about 2 hours until doubled in size.
9. Use a paper towel or napkin dabbed with 1 tablespoon butter or margarine to grease tube pan. Use a spoon to put the dough into tube pan. Cover tube pan with plastic wrap.
10. Let dough rise about 2 hours until doubled in size.
11. Heat oven to 350°F.
12. Bake bread 50 to 60 minutes, or until top is golden brown.
13. Remove from oven. Let stand 10 minutes. Remove from pan.
14. Cut bread with bread knife into slices about ½ inch (1.25 centimeters) thick. Serve with butter, jam, or honey if desired.

Makes about 12 slices

15

Finding Meat to Eat

Before the Civil War, Southern families ate a great deal of pork. But pork and other meats became scarce as the war continued. Southerners sometimes ate fish instead of meat. Other times, they made what food they had look like meat or seafood. Cooks sometimes shaped a mixture of corn, eggs, and flour to look like oysters. They then fried the fake oysters. This food was common when meat and seafood were not available.

Soldiers had to hunt for most of the meat they ate. Fresh meat was a rare find and a great treat. Soldiers hunted whatever animals they could find. They ate squirrels, rabbits, frogs, and rats. Bullets became scarce later in the war. Soldiers had to save their bullets for battle instead of hunting.

Confederate soldiers received a little pork, bacon, or beef with their rations. Army beef usually was tough and hard to chew. The meat often was spoiled. Soldiers usually fried the beef with other ingredients to soften the meat and make it taste better.

Confederate soldiers were inventive and managed to make bad food taste a little better. They flavored tasteless vegetable and rice soups with beef. Salt pork added much-needed flavor to bean soup. Beans partly made up for the lack of meat in the soldiers' diet. The protein found in beans provided soldiers with energy to march and fight.

"Off we go through mud and water knee and waist deep. Slept sound last night on wet ground and had breakfast of fat meat broiled in fire coals and ashes."

—*William Ross Stillwell, Richmond, Virginia, letter dated July 4, 1862*

A Grain of Salt

The meat shortage during the Civil War was made more serious by the shortage of salt. Southerners stored meat in salt to keep it from spoiling in hot weather. Many thousands of pounds of meat spoiled during the Civil War, especially when salt became scarce.

The South had never produced much salt before the war started. The Northern blockade kept salt from being brought into Southern states during the war. Confederates tried to find substitutes for salt but nothing proved to be a useful replacement.

Confederate Cush

Cush was a fried cornmeal mush. Most Confederate soldiers made cush from leftover cornbread. Soldiers dropped the cornbread into meat drippings. They added beans or leftover beef when they had them.

Ingredients
6 slices bacon
1 pound (.5 kilogram) beef roast,
   unsliced
3 cups water
1 loaf Confederate Cornbread
   (see page 13)

Equipment
Dutch oven or large saucepan
spatula
cutting board
sharp knife
liquid measuring cup
wooden spoon

1. Cook 6 slices bacon in Dutch oven or saucepan. Break cooked bacon with spatula.
2. Cut 1 pound beef into bite-sized pieces. Add to bacon pieces.
3. Add 3 cups water.
4. Boil. Reduce heat and cook, uncovered, over medium heat for 20 minutes.
5. Crumble cornbread into meat mixture. Stir well.
6. Cook uncovered for 5 minutes.

Makes about 6 to 8 servings

Fresh meat was a rare meal for Confederate soldiers. They had to hunt for squirrels, rabbits, and any other wild game they could find. This meat often was cooked in soups and stews.

Potatoes, Beans, and Turnips

Many Southerners planted vegetable gardens during the Civil War. Potatoes, corn, beans, and turnips were the most commonly grown vegetables. But many Southerners had trouble finding vegetable seeds to buy. Before the war, Southerners bought seeds from Northern states. During the war, Southerners saved seeds from vegetables they grew. Southerners sold, traded, or gave away extra seeds to others who needed them. Growing vegetables was not easy during the hot summer months in the South. Heat often spoiled vegetables before they ripened.

Once in a while, a generous farmer would give vegetables to soldiers on the march. Hungry Confederates sometimes simply helped themselves to whatever was growing in a nearby garden or field.

Sweet potatoes were a treat when no other sweet food was available. Soldiers placed the sweet potatoes in the coals of their campfires. Other times, they mashed the sweet potatoes to make pudding or pies. A little variety was welcome to Confederate soldiers who lived on hardtack, hoe cakes, and spoiled meat.

"We are five miles below Canesport, lying in camps. We have cornbread, beef, pumpkins and sometimes, potatoes to eat."

—Confederate soldier W. W. Bradly, letter dated October 31, 1864

Southern tables had once been full of fresh fruits and vegetables. But during the Civil War this food was scarce in the Confederate states.

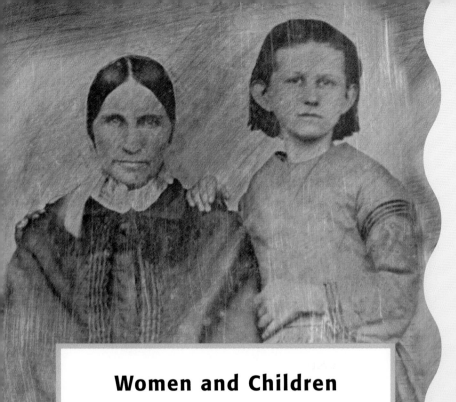

Sweet Potato Pudding

Ingredients
6 medium sweet potatoes
2 eggs
1 cup milk
½ cup molasses
1 teaspoon cinnamon

Equipment
vegetable peeler
cutting board
sharp knife
medium saucepan
colander
measuring spoons
fork
potato masher
small bowl
liquid measuring cup
wooden spoon
baking dish

Women and Children

The lives of women and children changed during the Civil War. Husbands, fathers, brothers, uncles, and other relatives were away at war. Women left alone on Southern farms had many duties, especially if there were no slaves to help. Women performed their usual household tasks, but they also planted crops, plowed fields, and harvested vegetables. Women and children took care of farm animals. When the family needed meat, the women and children butchered the animals.

1. Peel potatoes with vegetable peeler. Wash potatoes.
2. Put potatoes in saucepan. Cover with water.
3. Bring water to boil. Turn heat to low. Let cook 30 minutes. Drain water by pouring through a colander.
4. Preheat oven to 375°F.
5. Mash potatoes with potato masher or fork.
6. Beat 2 eggs in bowl with a fork. Add beaten eggs, 1 cup milk, ½ cup molasses, and 1 teaspoon cinnamon to potatoes. Stir to mix well.
7. Bake 30 minutes in baking dish.

Makes 6 to 8 servings

Eating Goober Peas

During the Civil War, both Confederate and Union soldiers depended on peanuts for protein. Soldiers often ate peanuts in place of meat. Peanuts were easy to grow and they stayed fresh a long time. Soldiers carried bags of peanuts with them to eat during long marches. Soldiers usually roasted the raw peanuts over a fire before eating them.

West African slaves brought peanuts to North America in the 1700s. Peanuts were native to West Africa. People there carried peanuts for food when they were away from home. West African slaves spoke the Bantu language. The Bantu word for peanuts is "nguba" (GOO-bah). Southerners heard the slaves using this word and began calling peanuts goober peas.

Southerners grew peanuts before the Civil War. At that time, Southerners fed the peanuts to hogs or shipped the peanuts to other countries. During the Civil War, food shortages forced Southerners to depend on peanuts, which were plentiful. Cooks put peanuts into candies and desserts. Families boiled peanut brittle in a pot over the fire, spread it onto flat pans to cool, and sent the hard candy to soldiers.

Goober Peas: A Civil War Song

One Confederate soldier made up this song after eating peanuts roasted over the fire.

Sitting by the roadside on a summer's day,
Chatting with my messmates, passing time away,
Lying in the shadow underneath the trees,
Goodness how delicious,
Eating goober peas!

[Chorus]

Peas! Peas! Peas! Eating Goober peas!
Goodness how delicious, eating
goober peas!

When a horseman passes, the soldiers have a rule,
To cry out at their loudest, "Mister, here's your mule!"
But another pleasure enchantinger than these,
Is wearing out your grinders, eating goober peas!

[Repeat Chorus]

Just before the battle, the Gen'ral hears a row,
He says, "The Yanks are coming, I hear their rifles now."
He turns around to wonder, and what do you think
he sees?
The Georgia Militia—eating goober peas!

[Repeat Chorus]

Peanut Brittle

You will need an adult's help for this recipe.

Peanuts grow underground and belong to the same plant family as beans and peas. Peanut plants grow about 18 inches (46 centimeters) tall.

Ingredients

1 tablespoon butter or margarine
  for greasing
1½ cups unsalted peanuts
1 cup sugar
½ cup light corn syrup
1 teaspoon butter
1 teaspoon vanilla
1 teaspoon baking soda

Equipment

paper towel or napkin
large, glass microwavable bowl
dry-ingredient measuring cups
wooden spoon
pot holders
measuring spoons
baking sheet
table knife

1. Use a paper towel or napkin dabbed with 1 tablespoon butter or margarine to lightly grease baking sheet.

2. In large microwavable bowl, stir together 1½ cups peanuts, 1 cup sugar, and ½ cup corn syrup. Be sure to use a large bowl. Mixture will bubble up a great deal when cooking. Use pot holders when handling bowl.

3. Microwave on HIGH 4 minutes. Stir.

4. Microwave on HIGH 3 minutes.

5. Stir in 1 teaspoon butter and 1 teaspoon vanilla.

6. Microwave 1½ minutes.

7. Add baking soda. Quickly stir until mixture is light and foamy.

8. Immediately pour mixture onto baking sheet. Spread mixture with spoon and knife.

9. Cool. Break hardened candy into pieces.

Food Boxes from Home

The typical Confederate soldier was an unmarried, 21-year-old Southern farmer. He had only a few years of school. He had never before been away from home by himself. Confederate soldiers often became homesick. Families and friends sometimes sent packages to soldiers. The boxes usually were filled with food and other small items available back home. Some soldiers even received big trunks full of goods. Packages boosted the spirits of homesick soldiers and gave them a little bit of comfort.

The packages held many needed items. Food was an important part of the package. Families sent sweets, breads, smoked meats, and vegetables. The sweets often were apple and cherry pies, fruitcakes, honey, and jam. Families packed butter, pickles, apples, pears, cheese, and nuts into the boxes. Soldiers in Jamestown, Virginia, once received a load of 300 live chickens. The soldiers feasted on fried chicken for days. Boxes sometimes contained candles, blankets, or soap. Soldiers also received books, magazines, and clothing.

Personal messengers often delivered packages to soldiers. These messengers were slaves, neighbors, relatives, or friends. They carried all the packages from one town to soldiers in a troop. In this way, soldiers received vegetables and other fresh food before it spoiled. Some families sent packages by railroad. This method was not very dependable because the soldiers often marched to a new camp before the packages arrived.

"The box had been sent from somewhere down in Georgia to some of their folks who were camped around Dalton but they never received it. The contents consisted of sugar, pies, eggs and plenty of other good things too numerous to mention ... Besides having plenty of good things to eat we had plenty of good old fashioned egg nog. It was a Christmas long to be remembered."
—*Robert C. Carden of the 16th Tennessee Infantry; remembrances, May 17, 1912*

The Sutler's Tent

Not every Confederate soldier had someone at home to send him a package. These unlucky men had to trade at the Sutler's tent for special treats and supplies. The Sutler was a traveling trader who offered food and other necessities to the troops. Almost every regiment had a Sutler's tent near the camp. These traders charged high prices for goods. But soldiers with money were eager to buy what they could from the nearby suppliers.

Strawberry Jam

Fruit preserves and jam were items that many Southern families and friends packed into boxes sent to soldiers. Note: Do not double this recipe.

Ingredients
1 pound (.5 kilograms)
   frozen whole strawberries
2 tablespoons lemon juice
4 cups sugar
¾ cup water
1 box (1¾ ounces)
   powdered fruit pectin

Equipment
large bowl
potato masher or fork
liquid measuring cup
measuring spoons
dry-ingredient measuring
   cups
wooden spoon
small saucepan
spoon
freezer containers with lids

1. Place strawberries in bowl. Mash with potato masher.
2. Combine 2 cups mashed strawberries, 2 tablespoons lemon juice, and 4 cups sugar. Stir well. Let stand 10 minutes.
3. Combine ¾ cup water and 1 box fruit pectin in saucepan. Boil 1 minute, stirring constantly.
4. Add pectin mixture to fruit. Stir 3 minutes.
5. Spoon jam into freezer containers. Leave at least ½ inch (1.25 centimeters) space at top. Let stand until set (not more than 24 hours).
6. Freeze, or store in refrigerator up to 3 weeks.

Makes about 5 cups

Christmas and New Year's Day

People did not celebrate many holidays during the Civil War. Southerners lacked the food to make big dinners. But they tried to find some special foods for important holidays.

Confederates always celebrated Christmas during the Civil War years. They made eggnog as a special treat. Eggnog is a drink made with eggs and cream. Even mixtures made with few eggs and a little bit of cream tasted good to the soldiers.

Back home, slaves celebrated New Year's Day with Hoppin' John. This dish is a mixture of black-eyed peas and rice. Black-eyed peas are light brown. Each pea has a small black dot. Slaves brought these peas from West Africa in the 1600s. The ingredients for Hoppin' John usually were available even during the Civil War food shortages. Hoppin' John was a plain and inexpensive food. Many Southerners believed eating humble Hoppin' John on New Year's Day brought good luck.

Southerners have different explanations for how Hoppin' John was named. One story says that children hopped around the table, eager to eat the food. Another story says it was a favorite food of a man named John. He would hurry, or hop, to the table whenever it was served. Other people say Hoppin' John may have been named for a busy waiter who served the dish.

Christmas was not the same for all Confederate soldiers. Men on the march near northern battle sites usually endured cold and snowy weather (left). Soldiers in southern areas often had milder weather, such as at this Confederate camp (right) in Corinth, Mississippi.

Hoppin' John

This recipe takes two days to complete.

Ingredients
water to soak peas
1 cup (8 ounces) dried black-eyed peas
7 cups water
3 strips bacon
1 green bell pepper
1 small onion, chopped
3 cups water
1 cup long-grain rice
1 teaspoon salt

Equipment
dry-ingredient measuring cups
Dutch oven (or large saucepan)
 with lid
liquid measuring cup
colander
skillet
spatula
plate
paper towel

cutting board
sharp knife
measuring spoons
wooden spoon

1. Put 1 cup peas in Dutch oven or saucepan. Add enough water to cover peas and soak them overnight.
2. Next day: Drain peas in colander. Pour peas back into Dutch oven or saucepan. Add 7 cups water. Bring to boil over medium-high heat.
3. Reduce heat to medium. Boil gently, uncovered, 1 hour.
4. While peas are boiling, place 3 strips of bacon in skillet. Cook over medium heat until crispy, turning at least once.
5. Remove bacon to plate covered with paper towel to absorb excess grease. Cool. Break bacon into little pieces. Leave bacon grease drippings in skillet.
6. Remove seeds from bell pepper. Chop bell pepper into small pieces.
7. Remove skin from onion. Chop onion into small pieces.
8. Cook bell pepper and onion in skillet 3 to 5 minutes over medium heat. Set aside.
9. When peas have cooked 1 hour, add cooked bell pepper, onion, and 3 cups water.
10. Stir in 1 cup rice and 1 teaspoon salt. Cover. Cook over medium heat 20 minutes.
11. Remove from heat. Let stand 10 minutes with lid on.
12. Sprinkle bacon bits over each serving.

Makes 4 to 6 servings

Reconstruction

The years after the Civil War were called Reconstruction in the South. Most battles of the Civil War had been fought in the Southern states where bombs and fire damaged many buildings and homes. Railroad tracks and trains were destroyed. In many places, entire towns had to be rebuilt. Union troops had burned Southern farmland and forests, which had to be replanted. Without slaves to work the cotton fields, plantation owners had to find new ways to make money. And former slaves had to find work to support themselves and their families.

Words to Know

blockade (blok-ADE)—a closing off of an area to keep people or supplies from going in or out

Confederate (kun-FED-ur-uht)—a soldier who fought for the Confederate States of America

declaration (dek-luh-RAY-shuhn)—an announcement

industry (IN-duh-stree)—manufacturing companies and other businesses

invasion (in-VAY-shuhn)—the act of sending armed forces into another country for battle

plantation (plan-TAY-shuhn)—a large farm found in warm climates where crops like cotton and tobacco are grown

pone (POHN)—baked or fried cornbread made without milk or eggs

ration (RASH-uhn)—a limited amount or share of food or supplies

scant (SKANT)—barely enough, or not enough.

secede (si-SEED)—to formally withdraw from a group or organization; in 1861, 11 Southern states had seceded from the Union to form the Confederate States of America.

starvation (star-VAY-shuhn)—the process of suffering or dying from lack of food

surrender (suh-REN-dur)—to give up or to admit that you are beaten in battle

territory (TER-uh-tor-ee)—an area of the United States that is not yet a state

To Learn More

Berry, Carrie. *A Confederate Girl: The Diary of Carrie Berry, 1864.* Edited by Christy Steele with Anne Todd. Diaries, Letters, and Memoirs. Mankato, Minn.: Blue Earth Books, 2000.

Clinton, Catherine. *Scholastic Encyclopedia of the War.* New York: Scholastic, 1999.

Dosier, Susan. *Civil War Cooking: The Union.* Exploring History through Simple Recipes. Mankato, Minn.: Blue Earth Books, 2000.

King, David C. *Civil War Days: Discover the Past with Exciting Projects, Games, Activities, and Recipes.* New York: John Wiley & Sons, 1999.

Wrobel, Lisa A. *Kids during the American Civil War.* Kids throughout History. New York: PowerKids Press, 1997.

Places to Write and Visit

Antietam National Battlefield
Route 65
P.O. Box 158
Sharpsburg, MD 21782

Confederate States Armory and Museum
529 Baltimore Street
Gettysburg, PA 17325

Georgia Historical Society
501 Whitaker Street
Savannah, GA 31499

Museum of the Confederacy
1201 East Clay Street
Richmond, VA 23219

United Daughters of the Confederacy
General Headquarters Memorial Building
Richmond, VA 23220-4057

Internet Sites

The American Civil War
http://americancivilwar.com

Antietam National Battlefield
http://www.nps.gov/anti/home.htm

Battle of Olustee
http://extlab1.entnem.ufl.edu/olustee/index.html

The Civil War
http://www.civilwar.com

Civil War Cookbook
http://almshouse.com/cookbook.htm

Stonewall Jackson Museum
http://www.waysideofva.com/stonewalljackson/

Index

10433